THE TEEN'S MUSICAL THEATRE COLLECTION

YOUNG WOMEN'S EDITION

W9-COV-204

Compiled by Louise Lerch

ISBN 0-7935-8225-3

HAL•LEONARD®
CORPORATION
7777 W. BLUEMOUND RD. P.O. BOX 13819 MILWAUKEE, WI 53213

For all works contained herein:
Unauthorized copying, arranging, adapting, recording or public performance is an infringement of copyright.
Infringers are liable under the law.

Visit Hal Leonard Online at
www.halleonard.com

CONTENTS

YOUNG WOMEN'S EDITION • NOTES ON THE SONGS

Beauty and the Beast from *Beauty and the Beast* (1991, film; 1994, Broadway). This familiar song is performed by the character of Mrs. Potts, and it refers to the overall story of Belle who sees past the Beast's rough persona and learns to love him. (He's a prince, of course.)

Belle (Reprise) from *Beauty and the Beast* (1991, film; 1994, Broadway). Belle, a bookish young ingenue, is enamored with Gaston. She fantasizes about who he really is and what their relationship will be. (She later finds out that he is a jerk.)

Diamonds Are a Girl's Best Friend from *Gentlemen Prefer Blondes* (1949, Broadway). Set in the 1920s, a good-time, material-girl flapper sings of what she perceives to be a girl's best friend.

Feed the Birds from *Mary Poppins* (1964, film). Mary describes to the children the sentimental story of an tenderhearted, old woman in London who takes care of the birds of the city.

God Help the Outcasts from *The Hunchback of Notre Dame* (1996, film). Esmerelda is in a church and prays for justice for her people, the outcast gypsies.

Honey Bun from *South Pacific* (1949, Broadway). Ensign Nellie Forbush is on an island in the South Pacific during World War II. During a lighthearted moment clowning around with sailors, she performs this vaudeville number to the delight of the listeners.

I Could Have Danced All Night from *My Fair Lady* (1956, Broadway). Eliza Doolittle has been taken in by Professor Henry Higgins in order to teach her proper English and raise her social status. She has slaved away for weeks at his phonetic exercises and finally, late one evening for the first time, speaks proper English. Higgins dances with her in delight. She goes to her bedroom and realizes she is in love with him.

I Enjoy Being a Girl from *Flower Drum Song* (1958, Broadway). Linda Low is a Chinese American teenager in San Francisco, and in this song, we hear just how American she has become in contrast to her immigrant Chinese parents.

I Got the Sun in the Morning from *Annie Get Your Gun* (1946, Broadway). Annie is a sharpshooter in Buffalo Bill's Wild West Show. The show has gone bankrupt and the only way to salvage the show is for Annie to sell her sharpshooting medals. Even though the sacrifice will be hard for Annie, she takes comfort in this song's philosophy.

I Have Confidence from *The Sound of Music* (1965, film). Maria von Trapp leaves the safety of the convent to become governess of seven children. She is terrified and uses this song to bolster her courage. This song was not in the Broadway show and was added to the movie version.

I'll Know from *Guys and Dolls* (1950, Broadway). Sarah Brown, a Salvation Army worker in New York City, meets a charming gambler and tells him of her ideal mate that she is yet to meet.

If Momma Was Married (duet) from *Gypsy* (1959, Broadway). Momma Rose has taken her children on the road in a vaudeville act. Sisters Louise and June wish that their mother would get married again so that they could have a more normal life.

In My Own Little Corner from *Cinderella* (1957, television). Cinderella has been abused by her stepmother and stepsisters. She finds her own corner of the kitchen, which is her only refuge, and escapes into her imagination.

It's a Most Unusual Day from *A Date with Judy* (1948, film). Not much plot is needed to understand this song. A group of teenagers perform a show for the community and this happy song is part of the act.

Just You Wait from *My Fair Lady* (1956, Broadway). Eliza Doolittle, a cockney girl, has been taken in by Henry Higgins. He is driving her crazy with language exercises. At this moment, she hates him and dreams of his demise.

Many a New Day from *Oklahoma!* (1943, Broadway). Laurey is a farm girl in Oklahoma. Surrounded by her girlfriends, she playfully claims that no man will get her.

Memory from *Cats* (1981, London; 1982, Broadway). This show is based on poems by T.S. Eliot. Grizabella, the glamorous cat "with a past," sings this hopeful ballad at the end of the show.

Much More from *The Fantasticks* (1960, Off-Broadway). Luisa is a typical theatre ingenue, and in this song, we meet her beguiling character.

My Favorite Things from *The Sound of Music* (1959, Broadway). In the Broadway show, this song is sung by the Mother Abbess and Maria. The Reverend Mother is trying to cheer up the young novice. In the movie, the song has a completely different context. Maria comforts the children in a thunderstorm.

On My Own from *Les Misérables* (1980, Paris; 1985, London; 1987, Broadway). Eponine, a street urchin, is in love with Marius. The relationship is hopeless, and she can only dream of a life with him.

Once Upon a Dream from *Sleeping Beauty* (1959, film). Sleeping Beauty is out in the forest among her woodland friends. Prince Phillip discovers her there and they dance this enchanting waltz.

Out of My Dreams from *Oklahoma!* (1943, Broadway). Laurey, a farm girl from Oklahoma, has fallen in love for the first time. Of course, twenty minutes earlier, she had told everyone that it would be a long time before a man ever got her. But hey, that's musical comedy.

Part of Your World from *The Little Mermaid* (1989, film). Ariel, a mermaid princess in the sea, dreams of a life as a mortal with legs to walk so that she can be with her prince.

People Will Say We're in Love from *Oklahoma!* (1943, Broadway). Laurey and Curly sing this charming love duet before they have begun courting.

The Simple Joys of Maidenhood from *Camelot* (1960, Broadway). Guenevere is on her way to Camelot to marry King Arthur. She is panicked at the thought of marrying a man she has never met. She feels she is too young to marry and longs for the "simple" joys that any legendary, medieval princess should expect.

Sisters (duet) from *White Christmas* (1954, film). This fun-loving number is performed in a revue as a "show within a show" in the movie. It should be sung as a duet.

Sixteen Going on Seventeen from *The Sound of Music* (1959, film). Liesl has taken a liking to Rolf, one year her senior.

Stepsisters' Lament from *Cinderella* (1957, television). Cinderella's wicked stepsisters, Portia and Joy, are insanely jealous of Cinderella's success with the prince at the ball.

There Are Worse Things I Could Do from *Grease* (1972, Broadway). When Betty Rizzo, a promiscuous teenager, becomes pregnant with an illegitimate baby, she sings this song to defend her way of life.

Think of Me from *The Phantom of the Opera* (1986, London; 1988, Broadway). Christine is a chorus girl at the Opéra Populaire in Paris. The prima donna, Carlotta, has refused to perform. Christine sings "Think of Me" as an audition for the impresario.

Till There Was You from *The Music Man* (1957, Broadway). Marian Paroo is the librarian in River City, Iowa in 1912. She has tried to resist the charms of Harold Hill, a traveling "music man" and con artist. At the end of the show, Marian and Harold declare their true feelings for each other.

Unexpected Song from *Song & Dance* (1981, London; 1985 Broadway). Emma is an English girl living in New York. After many failed relationships, she has finally found the right man for her, even after she had given up hope of ever finding him.

Wouldn't It Be Loverly from *My Fair Lady* (1956, Broadway). Eliza Doolittle is a cockney girl who sells flowers in Covent Garden in London. At the top of the show, early in the morning before daybreak, she sings this song with one of her fellow workers about a more comfortable life.

Beauty and the Beast
from Walt Disney's BEAUTY AND THE BEAST

Lyrics by HOWARD ASHMAN
Music by ALAN MENKEN

© 1991 Walt Disney Music Company and Wonderland Music Company, Inc.
International Copyright Secured   All Rights Reserved

Just a lit-tle change.

Small, to say the least. Both a lit-tle

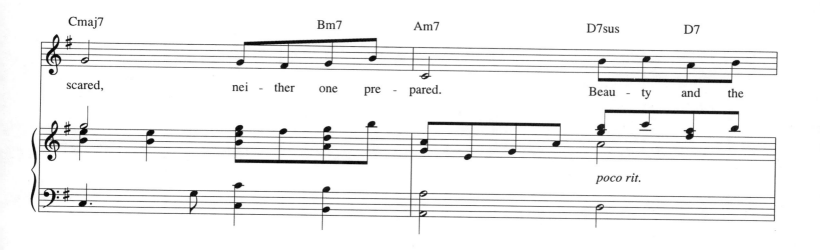

scared, nei-ther one pre-pared. Beau-ty and the

Beast. Ev-er just the same.

Tale as old as time, song as old as
rhyme. Beau - ty and the Beast.

Belle
(Reprise)
from Walt Disney's BEAUTY AND THE BEAST

Lyrics by HOWARD ASHMAN
Music by ALAN MENKEN

© 1991 Walt Disney Music Company and Wonderland Music Company, Inc.
International Copyright Secured   All Rights Reserved

Diamonds Are a Girl's Best Friend

from GENTLEMEN PREFER BLONDES

Words by LEO ROBIN
Music by JULE STYNE

Copyright © 1949 (Renewed) by Music Sales Corporation (ASCAP)
International Copyright Secured   All Rights Reserved
Used by Permission

I Could Have Danced All Night

from MY FAIR LADY

Words by ALAN JAY LERNER
Music by FREDERICK LOEWE

Copyright © 1956 by Alan Jay Lerner and Frederick Loewe
Copyright Renewed
Chappell & Co. owner of publication and allied rights throughout the world
International Copyright Secured   All Rights Reserved

Feed the Birds
from Walt Disney's MARY POPPINS

Words and Music by RICHARD M. SHERMAN
and ROBERT B. SHERMAN

© 1963 Wonderland Music Company, Inc.
Copyright Renewed
International Copyright Secured All Rights Reserved

God Help the Outcasts

from Walt Disney's THE HUNCHBACK OF NOTRE DAME

Music by ALAN MENKEN
Lyrics by STEPHEN SCHWARTZ

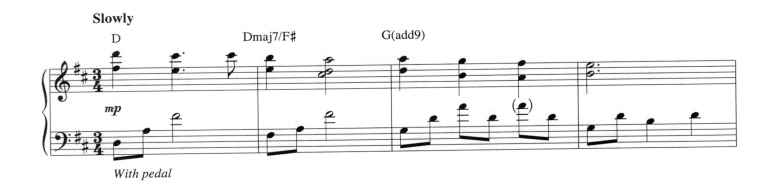

© 1996 Wonderland Music Company, Inc. and Walt Disney Music Company
International Copyright Secured   All Rights Reserved

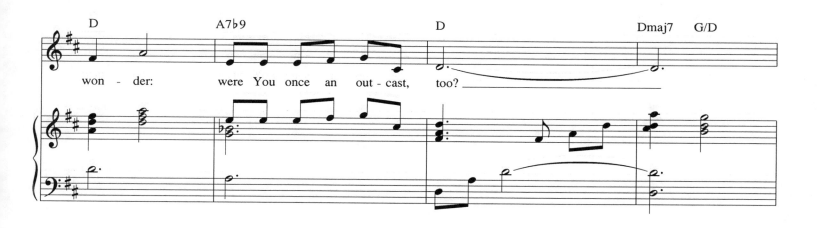

poor and un-luck-y, the weak and the odd; ___

I thought we all were the chil-dren of God. ___

Honey Bun

from SOUTH PACIFIC

Lyrics by OSCAR HAMMERSTEIN II
Music by RICHARD RODGERS

Copyright © 1949 by Richard Rodgers and Oscar Hammerstein II
Copyright Renewed
WILLIAMSON MUSIC owner of publication and allied rights throughout the world
International Copyright Secured   All Rights Reserved

I Enjoy Being a Girl
from FLOWER DRUM SONG

Lyrics by OSCAR HAMMERSTEIN II
Music by RICHARD RODGERS

Copyright © 1958 by Richard Rodgers and Oscar Hammerstein II
Copyright Renewed
WILLIAMSON MUSIC owner of publication and allied rights throughout the world
International Copyright Secured   All Rights Reserved

I Got the Sun in the Morning

from the Stage Production ANNIE GET YOUR GUN

Words and Music by
IRVING BERLIN

Tak - ing stock _ of what I have _ and what I have - n't, ____ what do I find? _ The things I've got will keep me sat - is - fied. ____

© Copyright 1946 by Irving Berlin
Copyright Renewed
International Copyright Secured   All Rights Reserved

I'll Know
from GUYS AND DOLLS

By FRANK LOESSER

© 1950 (Renewed) FRANK MUSIC CORP.
All Rights Reserved

I Have Confidence

from THE SOUND OF MUSIC

Lyrics and Music by
RICHARD RODGERS

Copyright © 1964, 1965 by Richard Rodgers
Copyright Renewed
WILLIAMSON MUSIC owner of publication and allied rights throughout the world
International Copyright Secured   All Rights Reserved

If Momma Was Married
from GYPSY

Words by STEPHEN SONDHEIM
Music by JULE STYNE

Copyright © 1959 by Norbeth Productions, Inc. and Stephen Sondheim
Copyright Renewed
All Rights Administered by Chappell & Co.
International Copyright Secured   All Rights Reserved

JUNE:

Mom - ma was mar - ried._____ If Mom - ma was

mar - ried, I'd jump in the air And give all my toe-shoes to you._____

I'd get all these hair-rib-bons out of my hair And once and for

all I'd get Mom - ma out too._____ If Mom - ma was

LOUISE: mar - ried. ——————— Mom - -

JUNE: - ma, get out your white dress! You've done it be - fore With - out much suc -

BOTH: cess. Mom - - - - ma, God

speed and God bless, We're not keep-ing score. What's one more or less?

JUNE:

If Mom-ma was mar-ried There would-n't be an-y more:

"Let me en-ter-tain you. Let me make you

smile. _____ I will do some kicks.

LOUISE:

JUNE: Sing out, Lou-ise!

I will do some tricks."

In My Own Little Corner
from CINDERELLA

Lyrics by OSCAR HAMMERSTEIN II
Music by RICHARD RODGERS

Copyright © 1957 by Richard Rodgers and Oscar Hammerstein II
Copyright Renewed
WILLIAMSON MUSIC owner of publication and allied rights throughout the world
International Copyright Secured   All Rights Reserved

It's a Most Unusual Day
from A DATE WITH JUDY

Words by HAROLD ADAMSON
Music by JIMMY McHUGH

TRO - © Copyright 1947 (Renewed) and 1948 (Renewed) Hampshire House Publishing Corp., New York, NY
International Copyright Secured
All Rights Reserved Including Public Performance For Profit
Used by Permission

Just You Wait
from MY FAIR LADY

Words by ALAN JAY LERNER
Music by FREDERICK LOEWE

Copyright © 1956 by Alan Jay Lerner and Frederick Loewe
Copyright Renewed
Chappell & Co. owner of publication and allied rights throughout the world
International Copyright Secured   All Rights Reserved

wait!_____ Just you wait, 'en - ry 'ig - gins, till you're

sick,_____ And you scream to fetch a doc - tor doub - le-

quick!_____ I'll be off a sec - ond la - ter, And go

straight to the the - a - tre! Oh, ho ho, 'en - ry 'ig - gins, just you wait.

Oooooooh, 'en - ry 'ig - gins! Just you

wait un - til we're swim-min' in the sea!

Oooooooh, 'en - ry 'ig - gins And you

get a cramp a lit - tle ways from me! When you

yell you're gon-na drown, I'll get dressed and go to town! Oh, ho,

ho, 'en - ry 'ig- gins! Oh, ho, ho, 'en - ry 'ig - gins!

Just you wait! One _

Amabile

day I'll be fam-ous! I'll be pro - per and prim! Go to

Saint James so oft-en I will call it Saint Jim. One eve - ning the King will say, "Oh, Li - za, old thing, I want all of Eng - land your prai - ses to sing. Next week, on the twen-ti-eth of May, I pro-

all I want is 'en-ry 'ig-gins 'ead!"

poco rit. *f a tempo*

Poco più mosso

"Done," says the King, "with a stroke.

mf

Guard, run and bring— in the bloke!" Then they'll

ff mf

Allegro marziale

march you, 'en-ry 'ig-gins, to the wall;— And the

king will tell me: "Li - za, sound the call." As they

raise their ri - fles high - er, I'll shout: "Rea - dy! Aim! Fire!" Oh, ho,

ho! 'en - ry 'ig - gins! Down you'll go! 'en - ry 'ig - gins!

Just you wait!

Many a New Day

from OKLAHOMA!

Lyrics by OSCAR HAMMERSTEIN II
Music by RICHARD RODGERS

Copyright © 1943 by WILLIAMSON MUSIC
Copyright Renewed
International Copyright Secured   All Rights Reserved

Man-y a new face will please my eye, man-y a new love will

find me. Nev-er-'ve I once looked back to sigh

o-ver the ro-mance be-hind me. Man-y a new day will

dawn be-fore I do! _____

Much More
from THE FANTASTICKS

Words by TOM JONES
Music by HARVEY SCHMIDT

Moderato

Refrain - con moto

I'd like to swim in a clear blue stream Where the wa - ter is i - cy

cold; Then go to town in a gold - en gown And have my for - tune

Copyright © 1960 by Tom Jones and Harvey Schmidt
Copyright Renewed
Chappell & Co. owner of publication and allied rights throughout the world
International Copyright Secured   All Rights Reserved

Memory
from CATS

Music by ANDREW LLOYD WEBBER
Text by TREVOR NUNN after T.S. ELIOT

Music Copyright © 1981 The Really Useful Group Ltd.
Text Copyright © 1981 Trevor Nunn and Set Copyrights Ltd.
All Rights for The Really Useful Group Ltd. for the United States and Canada Administered by Songs Of PolyGram International, Inc.
All Rights in the text Controlled by Faber and Faber Ltd. and Administered for the United States and Canada by R&H Music Co.
International Copyright Secured   All Rights Reserved

My Favorite Things
from THE SOUND OF MUSIC

Lyrics by OSCAR HAMMERSTEIN II
Music by RICHARD RODGERS

Copyright © 1959 by Richard Rodgers and Oscar Hammerstein II
Copyright Renewed
WILLIAMSON MUSIC owner of publication and allied rights throughout the world
International Copyright Secured   All Rights Reserved

On My Own

from LES MISÉRABLES

Music by CLAUDE-MICHEL SCHONBERG
Lyrics by ALAIN BOUBLIL, HERBERT KRETZMER, JOHN CAIRD,
TREVOR NUNN and JEAN-MARC NATEL

Music and Lyrics Copyright © 1980 by Editions Musicales Alain Boublil
English Lyrics Copyright © 1986 by Alain Boublil Music Ltd. (ASCAP)
Mechanical and Publication Rights for the U.S.A. Administered by Alain Boublil Music Ltd. (ASCAP)
c/o Stephen Tenenbaum & Co., Inc., 1775 Broadway, Suite 708, New York, NY 10019, Tel. (212) 246-7204, Fax (212) 246-7217
International Copyright Secured. All Rights Reserved. This music is copyright. Photocopying is illegal.
All Performance Rights Restricted.

People Will Say We're in Love

from OKLAHOMA!

Lyrics by OSCAR HAMMERSTEIN II
Music by RICHARD RODGERS

Copyright © 1943 by WILLIAMSON MUSIC
Copyright Renewed
International Copyright Secured   All Rights Reserved

Once Upon a Dream
from Walt Disney's SLEEPING BEAUTY

Words and Music by SAMMY FAIN and JACK LAWRENCE
Adapted from a Theme by TCHAIKOVSKY

I know you! I walked with you once up-on a

dream. _____ I know you! The

gleam in your eyes is so fa-mil-iar a gleam. Yet, I

© 1952 Walt Disney Music Company
Copyright Renewed
International Copyright Secured   All Rights Reserved

Out of My Dreams
from OKLAHOMA!

Lyrics by OSCAR HAMMERSTEIN II
Music by RICHARD RODGERS

Copyright © 1943 by WILLIAMSON MUSIC
Copyright Renewed
International Copyright Secured   All Rights Reserved

woo a wait - ing sky. _____

Out of my dreams and in - to the

hush of fall - ing

shad - ows, when the

Part of Your World
from Walt Disney's THE LITTLE MERMAID

Lyrics by HOWARD ASHMAN
Music by ALAN MENKEN

© 1988 Walt Disney Music Company and Wonderland Music Company, Inc.
International Copyright Secured   All Rights Reserved

The Simple Joys of Maidenhood

from CAMELOT

Words by ALAN JAY LERNER
Music by FREDERICK LOEWE

Copyright © 1960, 1961 by Alan Jay Lerner and Frederick Loewe
Copyright Renewed
Chappell & Co. owner of publication and allied rights throughout the world
International Copyright Secured   All Rights Reserved

sweet, gen - tle pleas-ures gone for good?_____ Shall a feud not be-

gin for me? Shall kith not kill their kin for me? Oh, where are the

triv-ial joys? Harm-less, con - viv - ial joys? Where are the sim-ple joys of

maid - en - hood?_____

mf poco rall.

mf poco più mosso

f

Sisters
from WHITE CHRISTMAS

Words and Music by
IRVING BERLIN

© Copyright 1953 by Irving Berlin
Copyright Renewed
International Copyright Secured   All Rights Reserved

Sixteen Going on Seventeen

from THE SOUND OF MUSIC

Lyrics by OSCAR HAMMERSTEIN II
Music by RICHARD RODGERS

Copyright © 1959 by Richard Rodgers and Oscar Hammerstein II
Copyright Renewed
WILLIAMSON MUSIC owner of publication and allied rights throughout the world
International Copyright Secured   All Rights Reserved

Stepsisters' Lament
from CINDERELLA

Lyrics by OSCAR HAMMERSTEIN II
Music by RICHARD RODGERS

Copyright © 1957 by Richard Rodgers and Oscar Hammerstein II
Copyright Renewed
WILLIAMSON MUSIC owner of publication and allied rights throughout the world
International Copyright Secured   All Rights Reserved

There are Worse Things I Could Do

from GREASE

Lyric and Music by
WARREN CASEY and JIM JACOBS

© 1971, 1972 WARREN CASEY and JIM JACOBS
All Rights Controlled by EDWIN H. MORRIS & COMPANY, A Division of MPL Communications, Inc.
All Rights Reserved

throw my ____ life a - way For a dream that won't come true. ____

I could hurt some - one like me ____

Out of spite or ____ jeal - ous - y. ____

I don't steal and ____ I don't lie but ____ I can

feel and ___ I can cry, A fact I'll bet you ___ nev-er

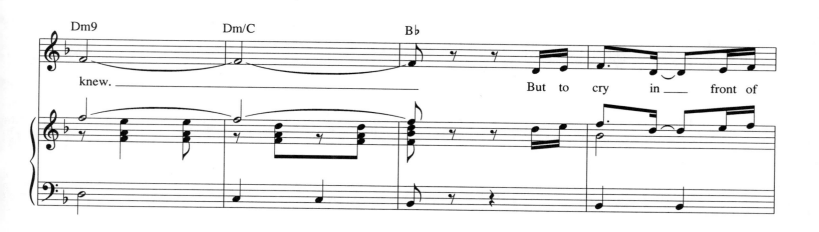

knew. ___ But to cry in ___ front of

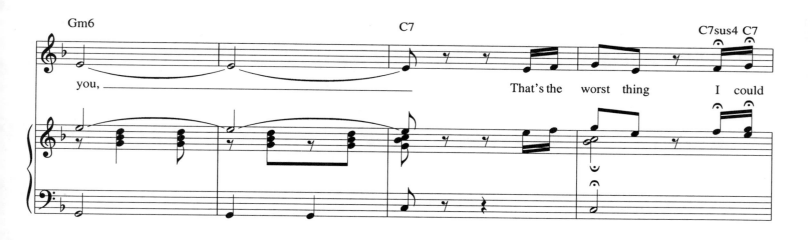

you, ___ That's the worst thing I could

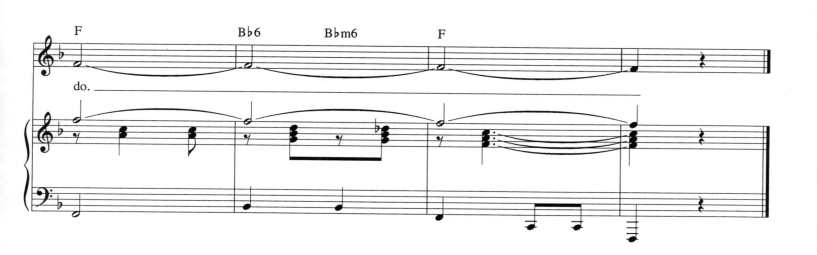

do. ___

Think of Me
from THE PHANTOM OF THE OPERA

Music by ANDREW LLOYD WEBBER
Lyrics by CHARLES HART
Additional Lyrics by RICHARD STILGOE

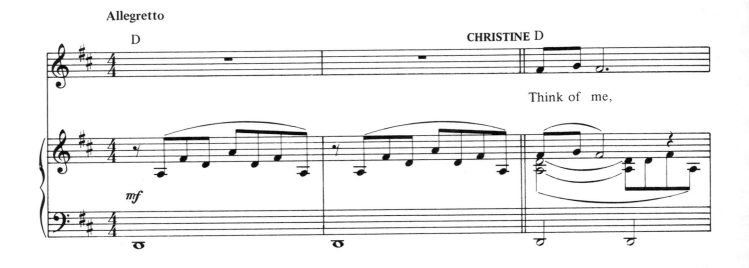

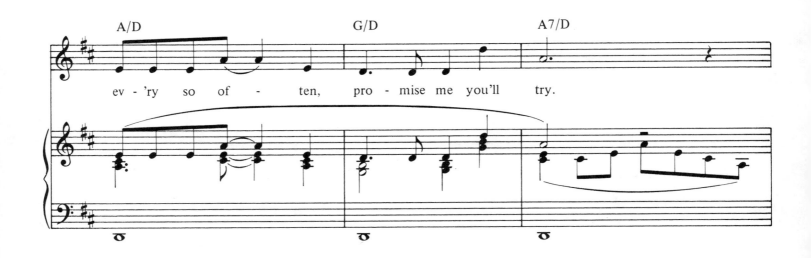

© Copyright 1986 The Really Useful Group Ltd.
All Rights for the United States and Canada Administered by PolyGram International Publishing, Inc.
International Copyright Secured   All Rights Reserved

On that day,___ that not so dis-tant day,___ when you are far a-way and free, if you ev-er find a mo-ment, spare a thought for me.

146

Raoul's section may be an instrumental interlude.

Till There Was You

from Meredith Willson's THE MUSIC MAN

By MEREDITH WILLSON

There were bells on the hill, but I nev-er heard them ring-ing, No, I nev-er heard them at all till there was you. _____ There were birds in the sky, but I

© 1950, 1957 (Renewed) FRANK MUSIC CORP. and MEREDITH WILLSON MUSIC
All Rights Reserved

Unexpected Song
from SONG & DANCE

Music by ANDREW LLOYD WEBBER
Lyrics by DON BLACK

© Copyright 1982 The Really Useful Group Ltd.
All Rights for the United States and Canada Administered by PolyGram International Publishing, Inc.
International Copyright Secured   All Rights Reserved

This is not like me at all, I never thought I'd
I just can't be - lieve my eyes, you look at me as

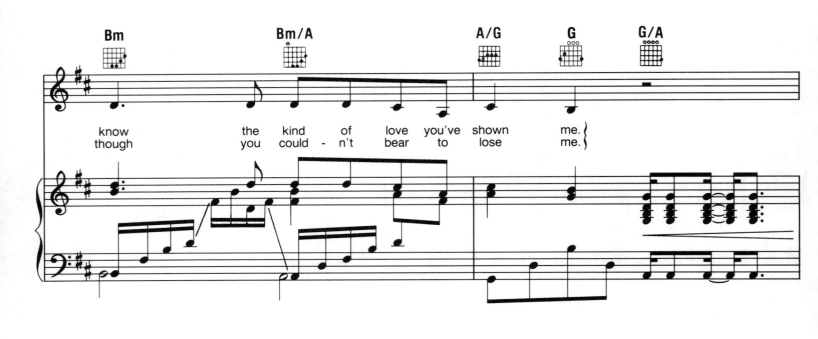

know the kind of love you've shown me.}
though you could - n't bear to lose me.}

Now no mat - ter where I am, no mat - ter what I do, I see your face ap -

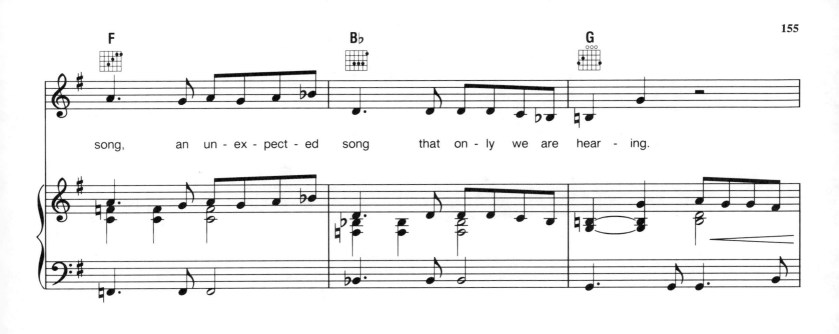

song, an un-ex-pect-ed song that on-ly we are hear - ing.

Like an un-ex-pect-ed song, an un-ex-pect-ed song that on-ly we are

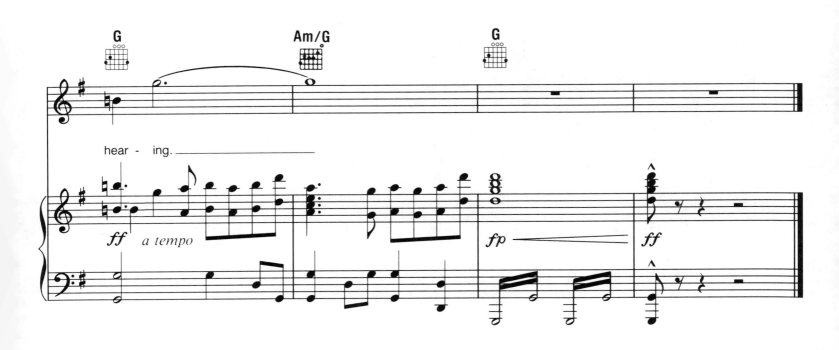

hear - ing.

Wouldn't It Be Loverly
from MY FAIR LADY

Words by ALAN JAY LERNER
Music by FREDERICK LOEWE

Copyright © 1956 by Alan Jay Lerner and Frederick Loewe
Copyright Renewed
Chappell & Co. owner of publication and allied rights throughout the world
International Copyright Secured   All Rights Reserved